Evidence of the Journey

EVIDENCE OF THE JOURNEY

poems

RALPH SNEEDEN

HARMON
BLUNT
PUBLISHERS

All rights reserved. Published in the United States of America by
Harmon Blunt Publishers
PO Box 250111 New York, NY 10025

First Edition
Library of Congress Control Number: 2006941007
ISBN-10: 0-9790005-1-3
ISBN-13: 978-0-9790005-1-5

Author Photograph: Steve Lewis
Cover Art: *Santorini* © Katina Houvouras
(www.katinahouvouras.com)
Cover and Book Design: NHB
Manufacturing: McNaughton & Gunn

For my parents

Acknowledgments

Poems in this manuscript have appeared in the following magazines, some in earlier versions:

CRAB CREEK REVIEW: *Easter; Tenth Anniversary*
HAYDEN'S FERRY REVIEW: *Early Spring; The Eyes of the Scallops; Peconic*
IN POSSE: *Bridge*
THE KENYON REVIEW: *Two Weasels*
NEW ENGLAND REVIEW: *Coltrane and My Father*
THE NEW REPUBLIC: *High-Ranking Fugitive*
PLOUGHSHARES: *Off Little Misery Island*
POETRY: *Continuing Demands; Double Nocturne; Estuarine; Evidence of the Journey; Horns Unknown; No River Road; Your Friends Have Gone to Florida*
SLATE: *Banish Misfortune*
THE SOUTHERN REVIEW: *Refusal to Level the Peonies*
SYCAMORE REVIEW: *Cow's Neck*
TIFERET: *The People in the Story*
TRIQUARTERLY: *The Revolver; Boatyard Mechanic*
WITNESS: *Eeling; Pigs Watered in Heat Wave; Stranger; Retirement: A Fragment*

"Evidence of the Journey" received the Friends of Literature Prize from POETRY magazine in 2004.

"Coltrane and My Father" was included in *The Second Set: The Jazz Poetry Anthology*, eds. Feinstein, Sascha and Komunyakaa, Yusef; Indiana University Press; 1996

"Hummingbird in the Moving Van" appeared in *Under the Legislature of Stars: 62 New Hampshire Poets*; eds. Agran, Crill, Decarteret; intro. Kumin; Oyster River Press; 1999

The author would like to thank the following for their help and support along the way: Joan Aleshire, Nathaniel Bellows, Marie Howe, David Huddle, Ilya Kaminski, Wyatt Prunty, Dave Smith, Ellen Bryant Voigt, and especially Gwen—there from the start.

Contents

Contents

Questo ripete il flutto in sua furia incomposta,
e questo ridice il filo della bonaccia.

EUGENIO MONTALE
from *Mediterraneo*

This, the restless rage of the surf keeps saying,
this, the whispering calm repeats.

I

Two Weasels

The first on a granite slab
making off with my bacon, my bait
for pickerel. All I probably thought,
fourteen and lonely, was, *That fucker*
took what's mine. Mid April, snowflakes fell
as gaudy as my lures into the pond's black oil
without a sound . . . treble hooks, fur
and hammered metal, now the meat was gone.

Then just the other day, the second, in a culvert
by the school, rusty velvet hose uncoiling
down the bank, a mouse limp
in the white thorns of its teeth.
It looked at me over its shoulder, then sprang
into the current. *Someone's*
uncalculated loss? For days
I'd hesitated to write this down.

Coltrane and My Father

Late one night I hear his breath
between runs, something the mikes
couldn't hide, what vinyl
makes us forget: the man
behind the instrument. My father
had seen him once, said that on a solo
he went too far out and never came back.
People started leaving.

Across the room the tiny lights
of the tape deck blink in sympathy
with the horn's voice, but register
nothing when he pauses to inhale, or sigh
with sudden joy, fatigue, disbelief.

A home movie: the barren, snowless slope
at Squaw Valley, summer, 1961;
my mother grows smaller
as a swinging chairlift carries her
and the infant in her arms
slowly into invisibility, and for a moment,
a stream of blue cigarette smoke
glides in front of the camera
from nowhere,
then out of sight to the left.

Easter Dinner, Flushing 1966

Everybody there smoked except for us,
and our father's father, who'd smoked for years
but quit. Before dessert we asked my aunt
for one. She passed it through the flowers lit.
I held it while my sister stretched her napkin
across the half-filled water glass, then wet
the edge and tore around the rim until
it was a drum where my dad put a dime
and we took turns burning holes around it
—the one who made it fall, the loser. We
faked short drags while the grown ups talked. A cloud
hung above the meal and I looked along
their elbows, plates, lighters, and misty faces,
and the face on the coin, too, vague and slipping.

The Revolver

Snub-nosed and black, with a polished wooden grip,
it came from her pocketbook in blue-veined hands.
My aunt's police revolver, a guest at any meal;
she'd show it to the children gathered by her chair
until my father made her put it back.
She only used it at the range, she'd said.
At her death it's what the lawyer came for first
and no one in the family kept him from it.

In summer, she'd swim while I pawed through her bag:
apple, lotion, the trigger like a tooth.
Eyeing rubber cap to the buoy and back,
I spun the chamber. Terns leapt from pylons,
fiddler crabs flinched by holes. She waded ashore,
sat and smoked, wiping my prints from the barrel.

Peconic

"The 1935 Thorndike-Century Junior Dictionary, intended for children between the ages of ten and fifteen—the age when children start to relish exploring by themselves—defines landscape as 'a view of the land' and 'picture showing a land scene,' but is silent about seascape, perhaps with good reason."

John R. Stilgoe, A SHALLOW WATER DICTIONARY

I.

Driftwood pylons driven
into bay's floor, with mesh
stretched between. Seaweed
tatters at waterline, rescue
notes ignored, forgotten.
We dreamt of throes, the entangled
collected while we slept.

II.

The word *tentacle* wrapped us
in the thriving water
Fish with wings and legs,
stilettos, mythic spurs.
We swam with sneakers. Once
you trod the horseshoe crab
you'd never grow again.

III.

Jeans hardened on the line
like garments of the drowned.
Salt corroded zippers
and turned the rivets green.
Pockets bulged with violet
shells, worthless (currency,
we'd heard, before our time).

IV.

Oracle of damp recesses,
the outdoor shower's stubborn,
voyeuristic toad, married
to the leaking copper. Hot
wind across the threshold
from burnt lawn, despite her
auguries of mold and shame.

V.

Poacher's remnants beneath
the red question: poison
ivy wrapping scrub oak.
Like quotations, deer legs
severed in sand. Held,
the hooves replaced the hands
beyond my sleeves. My own.

VI.

Black men, orange rental
boats, their dangerous voyage
through the locks to either
white-capped bay. Marooned
on concrete, we pierced our fingers
on barbs of shrimp, released
bails to punish the bait.

VII.

Wasteland of broken razor
clams when the tide was out,
the lagoon was ruled by blueclaws
when water flushed back through.
Reproached by the spit's swollen,

shimmering eye, we waded
behind our nets' shadows.

VIII.

Blowfish in kitchen sink
inside-out. The glistening
bladder, burst with knife-
blade: what, once inflated,
deflected predators' jaws.
Hooked, it rose to surface.
We didn't have to reel.

IX.

Anchored in our inlet,
the dredge a Trojan horse
against the dawn. By noon,
derrick and scoop were clearing
sand, deepening channel
for bigger keels and wakes,
shark fins nailed to piers.

• • •

Memory cups what never
lives again. We knew
our place by necks, enclosing
bluffs, the brittle casings
around the dead; opened,
miniature whelk poured out,
the future washed to shore.

Memory as Photojournalism

Hair in her face, skirt too short, my sister
flunks inspection. In tears, but finger raised,
she flees the table and my father's nightly scowl
for the incense he calls *cat piss* in the flaring
sanctuary of her psychedelic room . . .

LBJ already snapped hoisting
his stunned beagle by its ears; Diem's
Saigon police long since armed
with extinguishers to stifle Buddhist monks
who've dared to set themselves on fire.

On the smoldering front lines
of the home front, I am taking it
all in. If I owned a helmet, I would
remove it now, tuck it in the crook
of my arm, an apron of cameras
across my chest, free hand wiping a brow
then holding a peace sign to the future.
The caption: two fingers asking
for two more rolls of film.

Estuarine

". . . a shimmer of errors"

Vladimir Nabokov

Searching for the buoy,
my father swore and swept
his flashlight, illuminating
belly, wingslap. A heron,
knee-deep, exploded from
our prow. Night replaced
the olive twilight, and because
the tide had fled we saw
the river for what it was,
a feeble channel plying
the far bank. Our argument
was lost across the marshes.
In that trickle he could do
nothing but light his damp
cigarettes, which one day
would leave him drowning
in his single lung. If only
I could shun the perfunctory
metaphors of collision, and the waters
hadn't rammed beneath us,
coaxing our keel from gravel.
If only the brackish years
hadn't borne us past
the anger, through the inlet
to the complacent bay,
we might have wedged there
a few more hours, our
propeller spitting mud
into moonlight until
the shearing pin was sheared—
precautionary metal, meant
to break before the motor can.

Shop

Banana-Hand Krauss—named
for the crescent paw he hammered
on his bench to rouse us from
our pathetic grappling hooks and sconces.

Although he'd lost it in the War,
it was more powerful than any sign
he could have stapled with his *good*
hand to the board: NO HORSEPLAY

OR LOOSE CLOTHING . . . the famous leash
of Sammy Campano's necktie caught
in the drill press, spun him to it
like a yo-yo or reluctant lover;

and Bennett Watson's thumb smoking
in the purple bolt of the spot welder,
a junebug crackling in our neighbor's
tireless zapper. That teacher's stump

was more a drum stick (from turkey *or*
for snare), which could snug an ash scoop's
stubborn handle in the vise
and bend it back into a question

which had no answer. Silence around him,
spurs and flecks of silver falling
to his boots, he taught us to hone
our broken files into dangerous blades.

Apologia

A spilt quiver, the lampreys, more
eel than fish, settled in eddies
because I'd flogged their smug immunity
to the bronze current with my broken
hockey stick, bashed my wavering self,
Narcissus and Maenad in cut-offs, sneakers,
until I'd left a trail of floating
bodies, golden undersides bobbing
between bulrush, lily, left them
like the river's roadside trash.
               My
parents must have cupped their hands at
temples to watch me then, a lone
jet, some miracle of flight, vector
of vapor fading like a promise,
turbulence certain but imperceptible
at such a distance. With zits, a blis-
ter in the corner of my mouth, I
pawed my father's war books like comics,
frenzied for pictures, worse than anything
I dared to visit on the lives at hand,
my life an assault on anything incapable
of fighting back; because
                    I'd slipped
between the wars, I made my own,
studied Irwin Rommel's cold sore,
conspicuous whether he inspected ranks
or maps, extrapolating triumph, even
as half a man, goggled, unself-
conscious torso in the turret
of his Panzer, that dogging blemish
as much a signature as the binoculars,
around his neck. *The Desert Fox,*
who nearly won the war in Africa
but not at Normandy, who loved his country,
family, and killed himself when asked,
a complicated soldier with a conscience,
a scab beneath his lip.
               Another
chapter had Allied troops supervising

Nazis who lugged corpses from camps
to heave them to the pits. The camera
stopped the snowflakes drifting between
the racks and racks of striped livery
stripped from bodies, waiting to be
filled again. All those empty collars,
sleeves. Even though the flurry itself
seemed predisposed to stasis, to absence
of color,
            it was easy imagining
turquoise, Pacific blue, translucent
beneath the bows of landing crafts,
sloshing the dead Marines, face down,
helmets overturned in surf like
turtles. I searched for gun muzzles
in gray and wind-torn palms,
                       the way
I did each night as troops debarked
or loaded stretchers beneath the blurred
and silent rotors, voice of the anchorman,
my mother's complaints from the kitchen.
I remember regretting being
born a man, then wondering which was
more frightening: giving birth or
being the child in some paddy
with a gun? But the draft was churning
beyond my year, a wave's departing
back; you watch it leaving, relieved
it hasn't crushed you to the bar,
and disappointed to find yourself
unpunished, buoyant, safe, abandoned
by volition.
            Now, the breakers at Pointe
du Hoc seem uncomfortable edging
closer to German bunkers, chunks of
sunken concrete, like heads of shattered
Gorgons, iron reinforcement rods
snaking to the sun. A gesture of razor
wire can't keep us from the pillboxes'
tang of urine, graffiti, the damp

echoes of our own steps. Children
tumble to troughs, the meadow's velvet
craters. Our son wants his photo
with the Rangers' obelisk on
the crumbling verge. Reverent, stern,
and thirteen forever in black and white,
he'll stand between us and the half-
hearted cordoning of cliffs arrested
in slow erosion, the horizon's grainy
showers frozen at sea.
                                    At home
adults assumed it was compassion
that kept me hovering over a shoebox
stuffed with landscape, tufts of grass,
gravel I'd gathered from around the nests
of scything terns, the sky around
my head alive with warning, complaint.
It wasn't to destroy that beauty but
to own it, admire the weightless architecture
on my terms, place finger to orange
beak, the breast impossibly white.
The bird lay stunned, one-winged,
asymmetrical in the hot dune,
the rock I'd thrown to bring it down
colored and shaped like the camouflaged
eggs in clefts as subtle as careless
footprints.
                    Diminished, flaccid, the dead
lampreys had drifted past my ankles
schooling like ghosts to lodge in rocks
or be swept back to salt. I lifted
one to see its teeth, concentric
in the vicious hole. I knew they hurt
the larger fish, bored into trout
to drain them, arrows with wakes, and bent
for me, determined, parasitic, built
to fasten. But how could I have known
they weren't aiming themselves, or homing
in on kindred ugliness, were pulled
instead past me through rapids up-

Apologia

stream by something they couldn't
                              remember?
Seventeen years before my birth,
before we fell back to the world,
the circle of pitchforks, rakes, the other
battles survived, my father hung
poised above the bomb bay of his
flaming plane, the crew's receding
parachutes flattened into coins
among the bursting flak, entreaties
he might have emptied from his pockets
to fortune's shallow pool. If this
is my creation myth, everything
began with the sudden absence of smoke,
a descent that was the purest wager
of headlong flight, jerking pivot,
negotiations of silk and wind.

Cow's Neck

"It isn't easy to turn your back on the past. It isn't something you
can decide to do just like that. It is something you have to arm
yourself for. . ."

V. S. Naipaul

With a bucksaw raised above his head
in surrender, he waded from my view
to where waves chewed the ankles of driftwood
mountains. He'd turn the stumps to lamp
bases, rip the planks to picture frames,
gifts for relatives, but most of it stayed
a dusty knot of bleached and broken trees
in our garage, something that could reach
and grab you if you were small, keep you from
the bike or shovel, the clam rake or net
you really needed.
    In '65 I wouldn't
follow him to shore. Instead, I'd wait
in the bow, paralyzed, struggling to watch
him work between the intermittent backs
of lurching waves, sawing and dragging the limbs
to his pile. He set the tangled rafts afloat
then heaved them to the pitching rump of the boat
until I could barely see the white skull
of the engine cover beneath.
      This father,
the downed pilot, sprung from Baltic stalag
to wander a strange road home through many
kinds of freedom: the bodies bulldozed down
to common graves; the blanket-swaddled soldiers
staring from cold benches out to sea—
Atlantic City boardwalk rattling with traffic
of wheelchairs, the legless on crutches, the crazed
and shuffling whole.
      Why did we return
each year to the horrible point of land
where the beach was choked by interlocked arms
of rotting pine and eroded oak? Why
use days of vacation to dismantle, import
that refuse to our home, hide it in rafters

or in the corner by a broken mower,
posthole digger, and the rest? His burned,
wet back and shoulders still whirl away
from me in foam and confusion, in water
mean as memory, cut, drifting, liberated.

Split Rock

High as a barn, cloven like the balls of lead
we crimped to fishing lines. From the top
we pissed into its chasm, could see the orange
roof of Howard Johnson's where our sisters
waited tables. *Laredo* was the name
of the machine that rolled our cigarettes,
rifle bolt action, butts like chambered bullets.
Deerflies hazed us as we tore a magazine,

fighting for photos of the Lunar Module,
skeletal like our nearby treehouse, 2 x 4's
within the pine's inverted tripod (now
wrenched apart?). Other pictures: bootprints
in talc, a helmet's black visor reflecting terrain
where nothing was likely to happen again.

II

Horns Unknown

I.

Years of polishing and polishing the engine.
The fires never came. Sometimes the parade,
maybe a false alarm. Volunteering
had given me the luxury of conviction
on weekends, though other days I slalomed
fellow commuters as if I were the only one
with a destination worth reaching,
their complacency a kind of scaffold
I clambered at my leisure. *I know
where this is going* was a prayer I rattled
like a pope while watching the world slip
into a coma as if it were something more
comfortable.
How I longed to be the hero,
some instrument of argument, belting the soundtrack
of determination at the finish, aria
of spindrift, a victim enduring intractable seas.
What story would beat me to the future,
emblazoned on its panels and pillars like
reprinted posters for a tired film?
Instead, the trees keep emptying their arms
of snow, hold them out for more. And life
keeps falling to my shoulders, sifting brittle
hydrangeas, tibia of lilac, down the impervious
bronze puttees of the statue in the park
who suggests a world where every person dies
with a purpose. The silhouette of a flag
is any flag.

II.

It doesn't matter who
that waitress was—or is—clearing glasses
at The Vanguard, chime of spoon on saucer
unintentionally archival with Evans's "My
Man's Gone Now" as he leaned into the cockpit
of his chords. The origins of breath behind

brass on Montgomery's "Willow Weep for Me":
apologetic patina of *Horns Unknown*,
liner notes more kind
                              than this sky
at the end of November, an iron mask slowly
bolted into place, the clouds stacked
like blocks of granite ready for the finishing
stroke of the mason's trowel. Instead of crying
For the love of god! I imagine my family
backing out of fish market or pharmacy
into the path of a large truck, to hope
it will shrink the likelihood, separate fear
farther from event, make certain incidents
too coincidental. But I do this believing
somewhere it *is* happening, to someone else,
as surely as I know that somewhere two
people are screwing, in some distant country
the spikes of new cattails cut a pond's
surface,

III.

            and whitecaps pitch their tents, ready
the siege in a broad gulf where my many selves
will have to face each other, port and starboard,
no room for shoulders against the narrow transom.
Passing tiller back and forth, we'll learn
when to *fall away*, how to *reach*, or
what it means to be slapped *in irons*, cinched
in the vise of head wound head wind, a squall's
demonic pincers. Past the wrack of crab-
shrapnel, promontory's bleached mosaic
of broken mussels, we'll have avoided a life
of events like lower case letters rife
with nubs of entry, tails of exit to
the next. We'll send no dove to gauge
the closing shoal.
                        One day they'll come
upon our hull wedged inside the roiling

shelf, becoming reef, the rigging strummed
by viscous swells, the mast a snorkel tearing
mirrored clouds. Along the single timber,
luffing like improvised canvas, cormorants stretch
wings to dry above the veering glitter
they'll dive among, devour: a panel of experts,
unswerving students of the present tense.
Deck and rib collapse like blossom, plank
and stave elude their meticulous pitch.
                                          I've seen

the ancient harbor sifted, lifted from
that silt the fragments of tiles depicting dis-
connected hands (the grasped hilt in mid-
stroke without its blade, bowstring or lyre-
gut forever hooked on fingertip), along with
the unscathed amphora, its wizened grain of wheat,
lonely ounce of rancid, miraculous oil.

No River Road

It's a sharp left at the saucepan
with two bullet holes, white enamel
in parched grass. Once you're in, drag
the weathered saw horse back in place

then listen for the hissing of sand
on cinders and follow it until
the scent of evaporating rain
is nothing but smoke in the memory.

Trace the gorge, but don't expect
the boulders down there to be winking
back through blue green lenses. Any dilation,
current, will be your place in time.

Where there should be an estuary,
someone will be calling you
by the wrong name, leading you out along
the delta's arthritic dusty fingers

to make you an offer on his sluice,
his claim. At this point, empty
the talc and gravel from your pan.
Burn the paddles of the boat you're dreaming;

trim its sail into a flag of surrender.
The only water is wind-wrung tear,
the only gold miles back: like a single tooth
in the road's unshaven smirk, belly up

in the ditch, that hardened finch.

Vacation

"Germany has declared war on Russia.—Swimming in the afternoon."

Franz Kafka, August 2, 1914

Dusty cannons unhitched from their horses' backs,
the soldiers saddle-up and play polo,
mallets hefted, weaving helmetless
across a meadow of Queen Anne's lace.
And now, out of the shipping lanes, the U-Boat
ascends (misguided turtle in turquoise cove),
the crew breasting naked through black coral
or guzzling the wine of fallen coconuts.

Strap on the luggage, bring change for the turnpike;
the station wagon buckles, the tank is full.
Stolen by winds, that long trail of pink slips,
and every headline turned to fond memoir.
Let the front keep its charred trenches,
the punctured ship its fire, ecstatic sharks.

Your Friends Have Gone to Florida

where the Intracoastal Waterway is a sort of Styx
and the sun is hot, an Aztec sun with a tongue that's a blade
of obsidian, demanding blood and human hearts.
We've seen the postcards; the trees have leaves

like broken combs, and herons trail the walker down
the beach, no different than the brooding chatty homeless
who've decoded every punch line, the drifters who wait
for buses and never get on. Up here, where every winter's

different, the Promethean liver fills its ravaged cell
again, and we wait for another set of fangs to drop
from the gutter outside the window. It's the tide
they hate the most, these mill towns, unshaken visitor

thrashing the river's blankets, rumpling its neatly-folded
sheets of ice before it laughs back home to sea.
The birch in the park can load itself with as much
moonlight and snow as it pleases and still we'll imagine

the weed's follicle asleep beneath the drift, begin
mixing another skin of paint for the bandstand in May,
or long for a fleet of Harleys farting though the square;
we'll win the respiratory skirmishes as easily as this hand,

mittened, sweeps the bridge railing of snow and the river
turns it back to water, wrings it through the dirty sponge
of marshes. One more lifetime of wishful thinking,
a month of wearing whatever makes the least sense.

Amazonian Headdresses

In the glass box, without heads, long braids
of bark, the macaw's red spears, green cape of parrot,
black breast of toucan, and a single frond of eagle.
Malachite casings of beetle wings hang like bells,
shuddering slightly from the field trip stomping by . . .
this is worn at puberty
this one for marriage
In the dark carpeted room
a projector shows its film over and over:
canoes, blowguns, rustling leaves,
and the incantations of the narrator
thump above the whispering tribes . . .
Wayàna, Jìvaro, Mekranotì
But no headdresses, only silent heads hunting, the jaws
of laughing women squeezing poison
from gathered tubers. Howler monkeys, stunned
with small darts, tied tail to neck
then carried like suitcases.
And the birds are felled . . .
this one by a man
who has killed his enemy

Boatyard Mechanic

Evinrude, Mercury— the engine names
like epitaphs along the shelves of engine covers.
Outboards mounted around a dented rim,
shafts tilted in the drum's oily water,
black hoses uncoiled to orange fuel tanks.
Ratchets. Spark plugs. Six-pack of 2-cycle.
Tangled mess of cotter pins and pull cords,
shifter and throttle laid out on a rag.
Cold butts in the ashtray. Coffee pot off.
Gas smell, black sink. One black thumbprint
smears *July* above the cluttered bench.
Framed between strings of dusty propellers,
in violet spandex halter, *Joy DeCarlo*
holds the IM50 Impact Wrench.

Pigs Watered in Heat Wave

To catch what mustn't touch the sty's dried soil
they fight for the hose in hoarse, violent screams,
gasping, more than adolescent jostle—
their heads lifting snouts like shaking saucers.
Then the hush when each pig owns a shower
and all they've rolled in courses down their backs,
back into what they'll roll in late tonight,
and the black and white bodies start to shine.
Ears back, pink lips mouthing the drops and spray,
wet eyes shut among the swaying shoulders,
these funnels lean to the source, as if the sun,
dropping, were still a threat. In red dust,
the shit covered runt spreads his hooves,
braces far from the clear jet. Waiting.

Interior with a Violin Case

On the painting by Henri Matisse

The sunlight is a fork that hunts the tiles for more.
The vanity's black mirror is no different than the inkwell;
it won't give up whoever might be playing
or if something's even being tuned. The sky
is velvet that's seen better days. On this day,
we'll be seeing a little less of each other, thinking
about each other less. Below this balcony, a woman
will not turn to point at her children's fraying knees
and say to a pausing stranger, "They go through pants
like they go through milk." Walking beside his lover,
a man will stare more deeply into the orange he's peeling
for himself. The word *cadeau* will not be on our minds.
Today, we'll pass each other hunched, carry black
umbrellas along a concourse by the sea
and wait for the music that's nowhere in sight.

Elegy for Wolf Vishniac

". . . on the wave, water became bone"

Anglo-Saxon Riddle

I.

Life on Mars meant germs to him.
What he built would have caught them
if they were there—a vial like the pit
into which Odysseus drains his ram,
the ghosts of the underworld's valleys
swarming in to drink where summer air
is minus twenty, the fertile ground minus ten.
Project scrapped from NASA's Viking Lander,
he went to Antarctica for darkness, life,
for a pulse in rock and snow, to set his trap
where nothing should bloom, not even the frail
forests of lichens, skin around the stones.
In '73, the body and notebook found
beneath Mt. Balder's Plutonian slopes.

2.

Why look to the other cold planets
when the wastes are here at home? The boats
are on the bars, the clammers at work. Thin pools
reflect between clefts of sand, the sky
cut up, sent back to itself
in a thousand unintelligible phrases.
The tines of rakes dig in, cloud shadows
school with sunlight, the kelp uprooted, strewn
along the flats. Broken rafts of ice
are drifting, apology from the river's mouth—
bone on the wave, a trace of ourselves
where we'd least expect it. Vishniac,
the attempts are everywhere. Down the berm,
keel-grooves like furrows vanish in the surf.

Surfer's Eulogy

"... o'er all that glides
Beneath the wave, yea, in the wave itself"

William Wordsworth

All his paddling away was meant for return,
out through the breakers, then back, impaling horizon,
one hand lifted for balance but not goodbye.

It's hard above wave-noise to say goodbye
to someone survived only by churning horizon,
all that paddling away. He was meant for return,

so letting him go was easy; we knew he'd return
to us with the tang of salt from the horizon.
His hand (lifted for balance, maybe goodbye)

seemed to answer our waving from shore. Our goodbye
now? Out with the rip to an empty horizon
where all his paddling away once meant return,
his lifted hand balance, not goodbye.

Muse as Critic

This one sits at the edge of the paragraph
as if it were a mass grave, sprinkles another
fistful to the unboxed corpses of his bad ideas.

Is that a novel he's unfolding down there, or is
he just an out-of-towner fumbling with a map?
A poet writes of hand-rolled cigarettes. She loves

her smoke, breathes a useless aureole around the moon.
The old ones rattle past in shopping carts, in tanks, but when
will the young start paying for their meals, instead

of leaving only tips of rose petals, iron filings,
a pair of worn out boots? They tilt their ears
for the notes of bronze on bronze, but can't

feel the timbers of their own lives shaken
by the tongueless bell in its tired yoke above.
They miss the contrapuntal music, weep

for the fallen, yet flinch at scouring their wizened parents
in the tub. They make what they make to trap, but persist
with erasure, run the dead aunt's costume jewelry

through the dishwasher, twice, to rout the ghost
of cheap perfume, blind to the tarnished golden
brooches pulling down the little sweaters, artificial

pearls, planetary, slung like ropes of polished knuckles,
or animal teeth, about the white necks of the children
playing dress-up in the grownups' bedroom closet.

High-Ranking Fugitive

After *Most Wanted* was revised
as *Least Likely*
To Be Found, I went
to a film, and found myself
more captivated by the exit signs,
each letter a burning keyhole
beside the undulating screen
(Like watching the andirons
instead of the flames). How often
while hearing confession, addressing the board,
or in the froth of spurring
my deflated troops, had I imagined
a swamp peppered with wild iris, blue
as January stars? No one was less
entitled, more deserving.
But these are the days of the wide sill,
of sitting at the window. The days
of guilt are gone, when all
the running started, when every death
seemed stacked upon the next,
and I envied the neighbor's
daughter, who, recently severed
from her minions of threadbare
velvet animals, had for all
the block to see, taped FOR SALE
inside her frosted bedroom window.
I simply keep my balance beside
the cooling bed at sunrise
and leave the sheets the way they are.

Continuing Demands

I came to the tuba late in life.
First there was the draft, the tours of duty
then the welcome home. After I had combed
the confetti from my hair, after the coronation,
and subsequent abdication, when the crib
had finished its teeming and the deserted nest
echoed with the consultation of my own slippers,
the toaster ejecting its single slice of toast
straight to the jaws of retirement. I traded my gold
for cash, and apologized
for metaphor, was full of *as it were*
and *that is to say*.
                    Chained to his post
across the fields the prison dog is barking again.
I'd like to think he's happy with himself,
not asking anything of anyone.
The windmill in my yard is rusty now,
the blades are bent and shake instead of turning,
but not these valves, this fanning bell
which is the mouth always on the verge
of utterance, and which when coaxed
will flood the room
as blood will the polished chambers
of some struggling, desperate heart.

III

Eeling

You describe to restless kids
the man who's gone and grief
becomes the story: a beam
searches water and finds
the backs of eels in mud
before the eels can hide,
caught in the dangerous circle
of a flashlight's field of green.
What about the place? they ask.
The house and yard were a kiln.
The baked lawn smelled of sage.
Doves were bawling in the cedars,
and tiger lilies swept
the foundation like flames.
The world stung, as it stings now,
though army blankets kept
you safe from swarming gnats.
Your toes were on the fuel tank,
you itched to be up front
but he made you hold the throttle,
aim the hovering prow
at the silhouetted pylons,
the marina's orange glow.
He had sneakers, knotted calves,
a hand that held a spear.
The ring of nephews leans
a little closer as if
they see the glistening coils
lifted from water, shaken loose
in the yellow plastic pail.
A father's father, more
of a photo than a man
for them until they turn
the TV off and turn to you.
That's enough for now, you say.
But they're still cross-legged, waiting
while the windows crackle with sleet.
A family burns its bridges,
and the dead with silent hammers
build them up again.

Hummingbird in the Moving Van

Like a soul shot from a burning body,
she streaks from behind the stacked chairs,
past my head and the desk I'm shouldering,
to land in the branches of the mulberry,
not quite bird, but bee, or dragonfly.
And in the second before she streaks off
to work the orange funnels of the trumpet vine,
we face each other.
There is no imagined conversation.
I put no thoughts into her tiny head,
or words on her slim beak,
hypodermic, leveled at my face.
"What's wrong?" my wife shouts from the window,
packing tape screeching around her boxes.
I stand on the aluminum ramp, unable
to move, the weight of the desk bearing down.
I want to tell her nothing
is wrong, although my sneakers are slipping
and we have emptied our home again
to unload it an hour up the road.
Things could be worse.
I want to say . . .
                    It's going now.
Look, the lawn mower has made wine
from the fallen mulberries;
and the squirrels are hanging
by their back legs
to get the last of them.

Tenth Anniversary

A wave would rise, thin to translucence,
give a glimpse of something through its marbled window
then buckle into foam. What was it
we looked for behind those polished walls
before the world was there again
with its usual sky, its vapor trails dispersed
like bad ideas? Beneath an idling trawler, the bay
seemed an early morning parking lot again.

The three children, imagined at first,
now were here, the youngest
in her canvas sling upon your chest, pendulous limbs
swinging from the cinched, sleeping body. The others,
barefoot, dangerously underdressed
and shrieking along the farthest grasp of the wash.

Veterans Day had come and gone
and everything was elegy. The little park
was empty. The tangled swing without its seat
was a gallows with a noose of chain, the backboard's hoop
stolen from its tired bolts again. The monument
was new. We mistook it for a bench
until we saw the week-old wreath of roses at our feet.
Blown oak leaves gathered beside it made another cruder wreath
for the marble elbow to hold in its determined crook.

Growing wrinkles, the rollers balanced their final brilliant tufts,
approached like stumbling waiters with laden trays. And beyond,
the trawler tightened its circle, came to life.
Orange slickers, sudden cow-lick of diesel smoke
random as an artist's charcoal blunder, the cloud
of gulls vicious, crazy with hope above the rising net.

Still Life

Today she whispers, *I want*
to be Klytemnestra for Halloween,
the moment before he steps
into the shower, the place
where they least want to see
each other, and most.
Through the porthole
rubbed in the steamed curtain,
he sees upon
the counter her hairbrush
tangled with hair, opal ring
ablaze with green fire on the sill
above the sink: both as permanent
as Cezanne's apples beside the wine,
luminous of their own accord.

Early Spring

When the man from the hatchery fell, the net
he carried from the sloshing truck spilled down
the slope, and all who had been watching him
went scrambling for the trout, at least twenty
standing on their tails, swimming for the sky
as we slid after them and groped for smears
of green, pink, and silver in the thick mud
of our bootprints while slush the color of
coffee jammed in their gills. And one by one
we fed them back into his net and he
carried them to the hole drilled in soft ice
ten yards from shore, where he bent and dumped them,
a dull arc of snouts disappearing then
rising before slipping backwards at last.

Easter

Car full of luggage, lilies
for my mother's window sills,
my unbaptized children in ironed clothes.
These are the offerings before the arguments,
before her hand wraps theirs in church.

Along the aisles, the tilted panels, chapters
in that story of suffering: in one
a Roman soldier stands guard, aloof,
as another kneels, frayed mallet cocked
to fasten the figure down.

Someone else's children are crying.
The priest, his arms outstretched,
is pointing to heaven—prayers
flown up to the rafters, swallows
sealed in a barn.

Refusal to Level the Peonies

If they go,
there will be nothing standing
to frame the lake
when I sit on the small lawn
wondering about winter.
Nothing green, anyway.
And I couldn't care less
about the extra blossoms
I'll be dealt next June
with an Autumn pruning now.
They've been leaning closer
to the grass each day,
as if those fat flowers
were still weighing them down.
They're down as far as they'll go,
in fact, because the boxer,
my dog's friend from next door
after slipping through the hedge
and jogging two tight circles
around the buckling stalks
is lying on them fast asleep,
oblivious, out of reach,
her silver choker
gleaming orange
in the late afternoon sun.
She won't budge.

The People in the Story

which runs parallel to
but just beyond my own

own a pick-up truck:
blue, with rusted bumpers,
its simple cargo: three

golden boxes of hay,
baking in the dusty bed,
aromatic among the tendrils,

twine, and jumper cables.
All day, like singing
what crossed the radio's path

at the moment of my waking,
or seeing even when
I clamp my eyes the flash

of the brook trout's copper
prayer muted in the riffle,
I'll think of wearing the hand

that feeds the horse or cow,
or scatters thatch like a blessing,
a roof above waking seeds.

I'll dream of being the confident
man who strides away
to stem the levy's rumored

flow, to patch the subtle
damage of years with bundled
grass, to heft and shoulder

dead weight, clarity
that is neither grief
nor grievance, a body moving

forward, beyond labor
and love, bearing something
other than itself.

Banish Misfortune

Title of a traditional Irish jig

We are not out of the woods,
maybe in the wrong neck,
like birds intending stasis

who weave their clot of straw
in the grill beside the headlight.
When we watch the dog watch

the bee's hungry circum-
navigation of the apple
fallen to the fading

lawn, that burrowing amuses
us, as if the excavation
of imploded rot were somehow

different than the steam
rising from our coffee
or eaves of the future's sun-

lit mud room and rusty nail,
its retired blue collar,
bangles of expired vaccinations.

Retirement: A Fragment

There was a time he ran down the mountain,
fist clenched around the orange salamander
curling in its soft creel of ferns—Prometheus
and his ember, fire for the dark world
of the rented cabin, a mound of saturated towels
on the shining dock down by the lake. His children
bored inside and waiting for the rain to stop.
And then it's here—the bed, the body
propped on elbow, incendiary yard
outside, the boat out there
too, on its trailer, for sale and filled
with leaves, the blessed commuters
hurtling past . . .

Stranger

The benchwarmers squeal in their mattress of leaves
and the goalie turns her back each time
the net she guards surrenders to the ball.
The coach has lined the children up now, a row
of brittle flinching shoulders, every forehead
(or face) sending back the ball
to his waiting hands, one of which he rests
on your boy's shoulder when they're gathered
at the goal . . . simple congratulatory palm, fingers
of good will you think of the next morning
when you make his lunch for school, wax paper
creasing softly beneath your thumbs, flap
of a heavy letter he'll deliver to another life . . .
glowing kitchen counter, an open jar of mayonnaise,
your own father years ago, bent over his gift
of meat and bread, which unwrapped then eaten
at the beach, you tossed unfinished, paper and crust,
into the nearest can.

Heliocentric

The grandparents had run away,
so we chased them south to lobby
the congress of thriving palms

where the stars were reckless
sparks above the fronds.
Our train had traced its suture

from snow to citrus grove.
The rows of trees swept
from the window, a watch's second

hand. You were learning time
to pass the time. In your worksheets
the clocks were faceless until

filled with the sad features
of minute and hour. The train
hurtled toward the sun,

the sun at the center of
miraculous fruit which flickered
by, luminous, like traffic

signals before the red: no
returning once you'd committed
to the crossing, learned

the tenses, which is to know
age, that the aged
are drawn to the peninsula,

the continent's way of accusing
the equator, brazen finger
too close to the flame.

Bridge

In June, I pulled a sheet
across my father's face.
Now, on the river bank,
in late summer haze
and its contentions of sewer,
skunk, and barbecue, I watch
the evening current of birds
over the town, forking
past the dome, a gilded
boulder in their stream.
Farther north, the halves
of the new highway bridge
reach toward each other
like an elderly couple
across the space between
twin beds. This fall I'll drive
where I couldn't. A road
through the air above the river
where there wasn't one before.

Gestures of Concern

1.

My mother's father never showed his hands
in public: a mechanic's, tattooed with grease
and oil. Quick handshake, a scratch behind
his ear, then back they'd go, into pockets,
clasped diplomatically behind his back,
or tucked in armpits. Arms across his chest,
he'd rather squint at a passing parade, or swans
igniting on the broken light off water
in the park. When I was small and with him
in his car he'd reach down and pull the keys
from the ignition, the jangling mess of metal
landing in my lap. But we kept on moving
while he steered, one dark finger
curled and riding the bottom of the wheel.

2.

This morning a man in the playground sweeps
his metal detector over the sneaker-grooved
sand beneath the empty swings, pushing
aside their chains like vines across a jungle path.
I think he's waving, so I wave back
the way I do each week to another man
who cuts the lawn next door, who slowly
gives a tired salute before returning
to that rhythm of thrusting and drawing back
his mower between the cemetery stones.

3.

Parked at the beach, my mother sees my father,
dead six months, standing near the lifeguard chair
. . . blue windbreaker, baseball hat. And now
he's waving to her frantically. She leans
forward, squinting in the morning sun,
puts her coffee on the dash and begins
reluctantly to lift her hand. The night before,
she'd danced to the kitchen radio, convinced
she felt his chest against her cheek, then cried
and hoped the neighbors hadn't seen her.
The man looks beyond her toward the dunes,
where someone holds his frisbee, thrown there
or taken by the wind. He wants it back.

The Eyes of the Scallops

R.A.S. 1895-1976

In the cold yard, my children make a home
in a cardboard box, and I have made the same
of my desk. A knife hammers the kitchen board;
the Prairie sunset turns this room to rust.
In that silver bay, the Peconic, red-bluffed,
he was channel marker, or heron wading,
but from this distance, dragging the long handle,
he is a silhouette, any man . . .
                              The night
begins to shuck its pulsing stars, holds them
like the blue rows in his muddy basket,
eyes of the scallops in there with our clams.
We searched the bottom with bare feet, with rakes,
until the tide was at our chests, we worked
beyond this world's vague and broken shells.

Double Nocturne

Memory is like this mill town, sulking,
back turned towards its river, the purge and flux
of commerce always something before its time,
faces of the dead, face of the child grown.
                              There was a house.
Late Sixties, Flushing, 193'rd Street.
My grandmother filled the dinette
with smoke; my father came home there
from war. Red hassock, the bar downstairs . . .
                              I am always leaving
that remodeled cellar, its pin-ups illicit as the cubes
I stole from an aunt's Manhattan, sucked to splinters.
Through the laundry room, out to the alley
and immaculate stoops, my cap gun a pinpoint
in the sleep of dogs, that sudden bedroom light.

Off Little Misery Island

The bass we catch is too big with years,
its dark stripes notched and wavering
like a cut trunk's rings.
We drag it over the gunwale, stand back, and no one
will touch it, at first. The children cry
and want it gone. And when we do let it go,
it is not out of kindness, but loathing.
We are seeing what usually isn't seen,
the completenesses, the ends, the fish
trailing a red scarf of vomit and blood
back to where we pulled it from.

The white tide is nothing but time, crowding
the reef's rusted warning spindle,
sinking more deeply the reef itself,
and the bell in the buoy has not flinched
at its own trite plagiarism. So why are we most happy
when our lives are most visibly not in our hands?
Even when we can name the sea ducks,
or start the engine before the swells
fling the drifting boat against the rocks?
We knew what we'd find here;
we could see it from shore.
But that hasn't stopped us from circling it twice,
rounding every point, looking
for the single unrecognizable shape,
and the old shape of our lives
broken for a moment if not forever.
We coax it with lures—plastic fish
hurled into the wash again and again.
We sniff the air and sigh.

After thousands of miles of open water
the fish and the waves that carry them
must rise against the island's sudden contour.
From all that blue-black they must rise,
shocked, to a sanctuary of coves
and the testament of motion in sunlit shallows,
the strange sun on their cold backs.
But where is our world of new green foam,

the oxygen of effervescent sluices,
the brushing life of kelp and assault of barnacles?
The engine revs in a fit of blue smoke
and drags us backward off the rocks.
Water slaps the stern, fills the transom
and drains. We're out of trouble again,
drinking beer, talking of money, rinsing
in a fresh bucket the bloody pliers, the bent hooks.
And our children, trussed in their orange preservers,
are playing in the cutty as if they were home.

IV

Evidence of the Journey

After the search for the depression gene ended
in disappointment, after the failures of lens
and bench I went to the world, watching first
above tall grasses the white rumps of deer
floundering like the sails of small boats in trouble
just before they vanished into spruces
which ate them like a storm; listening first
to the timbre of crows' argument in drizzle,
then measuring the angle at which their legs hung
limply as they flew to the cities, where I traveled
from ward to ward cataloguing the scars of unknown
origin, recording the contortions of my own face
in the steel curvature of bed rails. What had I hoped
to gain? To shake the chaff from this drab bouquet
of data, crush the seeds with mortar and pestle,
toss them to the breath at the ocean's lip?
I was no different from the prisoner
passing time, carving the bar of soap
in the likeness of his guard.
                              I stood outside
the husk of Coventry Cathedral the way I've wished
I could outside myself. Within the cavity
of lacework and melted lead, a tatter of red glass
throbbed like a living organ in charred ribs.
The old man beside me was crying. He
was eighty-seven, had pumped water from
the shelters underground as bombs pounded
the city through the night. "In the morning
I could have cried," he said. And I considered
the difference between the consequences of violence
and the violence itself. His name was Morris Mander.
It was raining. I had my picture taken
with him. There was no roof, and rain
was falling gently inside the empty church.

Pham Thai Phuc, our neighbor's foster
daughter: thirty years ago, I marveled
at the X's down her leg, the healed incision
of fifty-caliber bullets. I'd heard her sobbing
when I spent the night, in her sobs the sound

of geese flying through clouds of driving snow.
Arriving or fleeing? What would exile be
without memory, if one could forget the place
refused, the place departed, and return a stranger?
Poker on the floor, whiffleball in the yard,
we watched her grow from walker to crutches.
She was sent back to her village before the war
was over,
              before the black levy was built
against the tide of names hers would not
be among, even though she vanished
more completely. Why have I searched its chiseled
list as I would a giant aquarium, its swarms
of orbiting fish, or a window at night, snowflakes
like sparks in the floodlight's beam? To say
mirror is only half the story. Standing there,
it was easy enough to ignore myself, to see
instead a ladder from a great height, the descent
precarious, impossible to read one panel's
human rungs, to say each life without
looking down, a foray into the territories
of drama.
              A friend adapting *The Women of Troy*,
cast refugees from the wars in the former
Yugoslavia, governed twice the people
needed for her play—a spare for every
actor; if one broke down, another could take
the script, continue—human bookmarks in
the spine of what has been, what must be
told again. Better that evidence than these
ticket stubs shoved between the pages
of my burning calendar, the perpetually obsolete.
Enough of the ancestors' clothes, which grow
more two dimensional on their bending hangers.
Let the dust settle on their brogues and boots,
the snow on brilliant maples.
                              Ahead, voluptuous
rubble, collapsing banks of wave and cloud:
welter of beautiful failures where the sun
has parked a rusting chariot to work inside

his torch's aura, lone welder perched
in the girders of another cold morning,
while I retreat into the convenient
shortcomings of my omniscience, like the un-
heroic narrator of *The Firebird* describing
the hero's progress, *I've no idea how long
he rode. You can tell a story in no time,
but it is another matter*
                                            to live one.

Notes

Epigraph translation, William Arrowsmith, from *Cuttlefish Bones* (W.W. Norton, 1994).

Page 5: John R. Stilgoe, from *A Shallow Water Dictionary* (Princeton University Press, 1994).

Page 9: Vladimir Nabokov, from *Lolita* (Vintage Books, 1989).

Page 15: V.S. Naipaul, from *A Bend in the River* (Vintage Books, 1989).

Page 24: Franz Kafka, *Diaries: 1914-1923* (Schocken Books, 1949).

Page 30: from *The Earliest English Poems* (Penguin Classics, Second Ed., 1977). This poem also owes a lot to Carl Sagan's profile of Vishniac in *Cosmos* (Random House, 1980).

Page 31: William Wordsworth, from *The Prelude*, 1805, Book II, ll. 426-427 (Penguin Classics, 1995).

About the Author

RALPH SNEEDEN was born in Burbank, California
in 1960, and grew up in Massachusetts and Long Island,
New York. He has taught high school English since
1983 in Massachusetts, Illinois and presently at Phillips
Exeter Academy in Exeter, New Hampshire, where he
lives with his wife and three children. His work has
appeared in *The New Republic, Ploughshares, The Kenyon
Review, The Second Set: The Jazz Poetry Anthology*, and
many other literary periodicals. In 2004 he received
the Friends of Literature Prize from *POETRY* magazine
and the Poetry Foundation for his poem, "Evidence of
the Journey."